Original title:
The Quiet Jungle

Copyright © 2025 Creative Arts Management OÜ
All rights reserved.

Author: Adeline Fairfax
ISBN HARDBACK: 978-1-80581-756-7
ISBN PAPERBACK: 978-1-80581-283-8
ISBN EBOOK: 978-1-80581-756-7

Mysteries of the Underground

In tunnels deep, the critters creep,
A shifty mouse, he's lost in sleep.
The mole wears glasses, oh what a sight,
While ants throw parties deep in the night.

The worms hold meetings, plotting their schemes,
Debating about their wiggly dreams.
A secret world beneath our feet,
Where even snails can't handle the heat.

A Lull in the Wilderness

A sloth on a branch, taking it slow,
Dreaming of races he'll never go.
Frogs sing ballads, croaks on the air,
While squirrels practice their stand-up flair.

A llama struts, his coat shines bright,
He'd start a band if he could sing right.
The trees sway gently, keeping the beat,
While critters gather for an afternoon treat.

Tranquil Reflections in Green

The parrot's gossip fills the day,
With tales of frogs that hop and sway.
The leaves whisper secrets, soft and low,
While fireflies dance in a twilight show.

A rabbit juggles with apples in tow,
And beavers build dams with a curious glow.
Amidst the brush, the laughter flows,
As silly antics keep the wild on its toes.

The Gentle Thrum of Hidden Life

Beneath the canopy, the mischief brews,
The badger with a monocle sings the blues.
The turtles race, oh what a sight,
While the spiders weave tales of fright.

A chameleon lost in a colorful mess,
He tries to blend in, but it's all a guess.
The quiet buzz of laughter and cheer,
Nature's laughter rings soft and clear.

The Calm Within the Canopy

Beneath the leafy green, a breeze so shy,
The parrots gossip as the sloths creep by.
A turtle in a hat, oh what a sight!
He's late for tea; it's quite the silly plight.

Monkeys juggling fruit, their eyes agleam,
While a slumbering snake dreams of ice cream.
Lizards play poker on a log so stout,
In this jungle carnival, who's left out?

Silence Cradled by Vines

A frog in a crown croaked a royal tune,
While butterflies danced beneath the full moon.
An owl spilled secrets but forgot the words,
As the chatter of crickets laughed at the birds.

In this leafy realm, the shadows sway,
The ants are plotting for a grand buffet.
A sleepy old bear, dreaming of cheese,
Wakes up to find nothing but buzzing bees.

Refuge of the Wilderness

Giraffes wear ties as they sip on soda,
While deer hold a meeting to plan a new quota.
A porcupine's knitting, what a quirky art,
Even the mushrooms join in, playing part.

Lemons rolling free in a tangle of leaves,
The mischief is palpable; the jungle deceives.
Bats on the branches giggle through the night,
Chasing fireflies, what a whimsical flight!

Shadows of Forgotten Paths

A fox in a bowtie tells jokes to a frog,
While raccoons debate over who's the best log.
A parade of ants marches with a bang,
Their route is a riddle; oh, how they sang!

Twinkling tails of a playful raccoon,
Swaying with rhythm to the night's merry tune.
The air is thick with laughter and cheer,
In the shadows they whisper, 'Adventure is near!'

Serenity Among the Specters

In the shade where shadows play,
A lazy monkey steals a stay.
His antics cause the birds to caw,
While I just munch on bamboo straw.

Lizards lounge with style so grand,
While ants march in a fine parade band.
A sloth swings down, and oh what grace,
He forgets his snack in a leafy place.

Still Waters Run Green

The pond reflects a goofy grin,
As frogs perform their ribbiting spin.
A turtle winks, then takes a nap,
While dragonflies play tag in a flap.

The fish in silver jackets glide,
They chase their tails with utter pride.
A catfish tries to strike a pose,
But sneezes loud—oh, how it shows!

The Soft Dance of Dappled Light

Sunbeams waltz through branches wide,
As squirrels scamper, full of pride.
A playful breeze starts swaying leaves,
While porcupines weave into thieves.

A capybara lounges, looking chic,
While an owl hoots, like it's peek-a-boo week.
A rustle here, a giggle there,
Nature's jokes hang in the air!

Calm Realms Untamed

The vines hang low like curious cats,
While a parrot squawks about the spats.
A cheerful chameleon, sly and bright,
Plays hide-and-seek in the fading light.

Bees buzz around like they own the place,
While a turtle's slow, but wins the race.
With every sound, a chuckle's found,
In this serene, silly playground.

The Sound of Stillness

In a world where whispers fade,
The creatures play a sneaky charade.
A sloth laughs at a startled hare,
While butterflies dance without a care.

A parrot tells jokes to a shy old frog,
Their laughter echoes through the bog.
A snake slips past with a cheeky grin,
Winking at shadows where silliness begins.

Lurking in the Lushness

In leaves of green, a secret spy,
A chameleon, grinning, tries to fly.
He blends in so well that you won't see,
His jokes are as funny as can be!

A tapir sneezes, rattles the trees,
All the critters giggle with ease.
The panther trips over a fallen branch,
And the whole forest joins in a dance.

Nature's Soft Embrace

A cuddle of ferns in a grassy bay,
Welcomes a tortoise who just wants to play.
He spins in circles, a slow-motion dance,
While a cricket hops by, trying to prance.

The flowers giggle when the breeze blows in,
Tickling their petals and causing a spin.
A turtle might tease a squirrel with glee,
"Catch me if you can, but I'm slow, you see!"

Gentle Footfalls on the Forest Floor

With each soft step, the ground does squeak,
A raccoon sneaks by, playful and cheeky.
He lifts a paw, then gives a big yawn,
As if he were dreaming of a new dawn.

An owl hoots softly, a wise old gent,
Cracking jokes from his high-up tent.
When night falls, all creatures adore,
The funny little tales shared forevermore.

The Language of the Undergrowth

In the grass, a cricket sings,
Telling tales of silly kings.
Leaves rustle, gossip's afoot,
While ants march in little suits.

Frogs joke with a ribbit cheer,
While spiders weave webs like they're here.
A squirrel jokes, tail flicking high,
'Catch my jokes? You must be spry!'

The Quiet Dance of Nature

A monkey swings with a funny face,
In a leafy, messy, wild space.
Butterflies flit with a bashful glance,
While worms try to join the dance!

The flowers giggle in the breeze,
'We bloom for the bees, it's a tease!'
The wind whispers secrets near,
As creatures burst into laughter here.

Serenity Lingers in the Green

Bamboo sways with a creaky sound,
While a sleepy sloth hangs around.
Lively lizards, they speed by,
'Catch us all!' is their battle cry!

The sun peeks through, shining bright,
Chasing shadows with all its might.
The world's a stage of leafy dreams,
Where nothing's quite as it seems.

A Breath Among the Fronds

Breezes tickle a tiger's nose,
He sneezes loud, then off he goes!
Parrots squawk in vibrant hues,
Sharing gossip while they cruise.

The jungle boasts its quirks and tunes,
As raccoons host silly cartoons.
With every rustle, playful fun,
Where nature laughs under the sun!

Prayers of the Verdant Realm

In the leaves a whisper sings,
A squirrel dons a crown of twigs.
With acorns dropped like silly things,
He prays for nuts, the laughter digs.

The ferns nod in their leafy grace,
As butterflies show off their lace.
A chameleon, in haste, misplaced,
Turns purple with the funny face.

Beneath the blooms, a beetle jives,
While ants in suits do business thrive.
They barter crumbs and shout high-fives,
For snack time's where the fun derives.

A parrot cackles, what a joke!
He mimics frogs and then a croak.
In this realm, where laughter's woke,
Nature's whimsy's quite bespoke.

Unseen Serenity of Biodiversity

In shadows where the critters dwell,
A sloth swings down, oh such a swell!
He waves goodnight, but it's a tell,
That he's just napping, all is well.

A spider spins a web so fine,
Declares it's art, a bold design.
But flies just laugh and laugh, opine,
As dinner served, doth taste divine.

The frogs compete with croaks of glee,
A symphony of silliness, see!
Each note a ribbit, wild and free,
Their audience? A sleepy bee.

Through tangled greens, a raccoon peeks,
With bandit mask and playful cheeks.
He sneaks and scurries, what a freak!
In nature's gala, joy peaks high.

The Timid Call of Dusk

As daylight fades, the fireflies glow,
With twinkles bright, a cosmic show.
The crickets chirp in sync, you know,
To welcome night with a friendly hello.

A hedgehog rolls, and what a sight!
He bumps a bush, a comical fright.
With spiny poise, he takes flight,
Into the dark, what a silly knight!

An owl laughs, "Whooo's the real king?"
He hoots and winks, like it's nothing.
A bat then swoops for a quick fling,
With awkward loops, he claims the ring.

Beneath the stars, the troupe convenes,
Jungle parties filled with memes,
All creatures sip on moonlit beams,
As dusk descends in gentle schemes.

In the Embrace of Solitude

In stillness, a snail moves with flair,
Carrying dreams with utmost care.
He laughs at the speedy, full of air,
While pondering life and leafy wear.

A lizard basking on a warm stone,
Counts tallies of how far he's grown.
With every puff, he claims his throne,
In solitude, he feels right at home.

A hedgehog sighs and rolls in peace,
His worries piled, he must release.
He dreams of journeys, sweet increase,
While tender moss cradles his fleece.

Oh, solitude is quite a friend,
With quirks that never seem to end.
In nature's arms, laughter does blend,
As moments shared, we gladly spend.

The Stillness of Mossy Stones

In shadows where the critters creep,
Mossy stones play hide and seek.
A turtle slips, with speed so slow,
While frogs debate on where to go.

The sun peeks through the leafy veil,
And whispers tales of a soft trail.
A snail leaves notes in slime for fun,
While ants march home, their day is done.

A squirrel grins with a nut so grand,
Thinking it's a treasure, not so planned.
While beetles dance a wobbly jig,
We laugh at life, it's small and big.

In this place where silence beams,
Laughter hides in daylight dreams.
With every rustle, giggles bounce,
In this stillness, joy can pounce.

Traces of Serene Life

The whispers of the wind make reels,
And dancing leaves spin joyful feels.
A lizard yawns, quite unimpressed,
While mushrooms wear their gnome-like vests.

A butterfly on a flower's head,
Clumsily tries its fame instead.
It stumbles 'round like it's in a race,
Fancy twirls in a small, tight space.

Caterpillars bring their own cheer,
Crawling up a branch without any fear.
An ant in shades, a tiny cool knight,
Claims every crumb, it's quite a sight!

In shadows where laughter and fun strife,
Traces of calm show a silly life.
Each rustle and giggle, a reason to cheer,
In this quiet world, silliness is near.

Echoes of a Secret World

In tangled vines, a chorus sings,
Of silly tales and secret things.
A fox waddles in, wearing a grin,
While crickets play a violin.

The old owl snores, a soft, sweet sound,
While fireflies twirl and dance around.
A raccoon peeks, clutching a snack,
His bandit mask, never lacking tact.

The moonlight chuckles, beams so bright,
Illuminating the quirks of night.
A wise little mouse gives advice on cheese,
"Take a nibble, do with ease!"

Echoes play tricks, their giggles soar,
In a hush where they explore.
This secret realm, a merry delight,
Where silliness dances and spirits take flight.

The Hushed Symphony of the Earth

Soft murmurs blend in harmony,
As tiny critters share their glee.
A plump toad croaks a funny tune,
Beneath the watch of a cheeky moon.

Grasshoppers leap like they own the show,
While bumblebees buzz in elegant flow.
Each note a giggle, a playful sway,
In this concert where the critters play.

A snail brings its shell as a drum,
Filling the air with a comical hum.
While worms do the twist in the cool night air,
All is calm, no worries or care.

As echoes linger through leaves' embrace,
The symphony of silliness finds its place.
In this hush where laughter rings true,
The earth whispers secrets, funny and new.

Nature's Unvoiced Requiem

In a forest where the trees do grin,
Squirrels giggle with acorn kin.
Frogs wear tiny boots, oh-so-fine,
They dance with glee, a silly line.

Pine trees whisper jokes, oh so sly,
While chipmunks throw pies, oh my!
Leaves twirl and chatter, a secret affair,
Nature's laughter fills the air.

A turtle trips on its own shell,
Crashing softly, oh what a swell!
Bees join in with a jazzy buzz,
In this quiet, funny forest was.

Stars burst out in laughter above,
While owls roll their eyes, oh how they love!
With every rustle and jolly cheer,
Life's hilarity echoes here.

Crickets' Chorus at Dusk.

As day turns down and stars reveal,
Crickets sing in a grand wheel.
With tiny instruments, quite the show,
They blend with grass and start to glow.

A grasshopper joins with a plucky hop,
In the midst, he slips, oh plop!
Fireflies flicker, in disco bliss,
Lighting up the night with a wiggly kiss.

The moon chuckles, peeking through,
As frogs join in with a croaky cue.
Worms do a wormy little dance,
Nature's night, in a funny trance.

Beneath the stars, all join the spree,
As shadows waltz and spin with glee.
The chorus builds, no need to fuss,
In this calm, wild world, all are a-plus.

Whispers of the Canopy

Above the world where the branches sway,
Laughter drifts through leaves at play.
Monkeys trade jokes, swinging along,
With a side-splitting tune, oh so strong.

The parrot squawks, dressed bright and bold,
In feathers of laughter, tales unfold.
A sloth, though slow, cracks the best puns,
His timing is like a tree when it runs!

Sunlight dapples, a theater of mirth,
Nature's stage for a whimsical birth.
With each soft rustle, a tale comes alive,
Where giggles cascade and funny vibes thrive.

Beneath the vibrant, leafy dome,
Critters find joy, making it home.
They share their secrets without a word,
Nature's humor, wildly absurd.

Shadows Beneath the Leaves

In shadows deep where whispers play,
Chimps in tuxedos steal the day.
They juggle bananas, a sight to behold,
With laughter so loud, breaking the mold.

A rabbit hops in with a silly hat,
Bouncing along, imagining that.
Snakes slither in, with a grin so wide,
Telling tales of the ones they've spied.

Night creeps softly, crickets ignite,
The moon winks back, full of delight.
Bats fly by, wearing capes of gloom,
Casual superheroes, in nature's loom.

Under the leafy, laughing skies,
Life's joyous antics bring surprise.
In shadows adorned with laughter's weave,
The forest rejoices in what it believes.

Enchanted Silence in the Grove

In the woods where no one speaks,
A squirrel wearing fancy sneaks.
He dances 'round the tall, tall trees,
Tickling leaves in the summer breeze.

Birds gossip in their own fun way,
About the frog who lost his sway.
He slipped on mud and took a fall,
The laughter echoed through it all.

A turtle slow, he's on a quest,
To find the hammock and take a rest.
But with each step, he stops to chat,
With beetles who wear tiny hats.

In this place where whispers reign,
A game of hide and seek is plain.
With every rustle, giggles gather,
Oh, nature's fun can really tatter!

Deep within the Foliage

Where shadows play and secrets hide,
A tree stump hosts a furry ride.
A raccoon dons a mask of glee,
He swipes a snack from the nearest bee.

The butterflies are having tea,
Discussing who's the best at flee.
The caterpillar, munching slow,
Claims he's the fastest, but we all know!

A lizard jumps with quite the flair,
Chasing his tail without a care.
The ants parade with tiny flair,
While crickets lead them with a stare.

Amidst the vines, the laughs grow loud,
As branches sway around the crowd.
Oh, listen close; you might just hear,
The forest's giggles, oh so dear!

Silenced by Nature's Embrace

In a nook where giggles bloom,
A rabbit hops, with zoom and zoom.
He gives a bow, then takes a leap,
As turtles watch from where they creep.

Bees buzz tunes, a lively choir,
While leaves debate who's got more fire.
A hedgehog rolls a tiny spike,
And claims it's just a magic strike.

A bush of berries holds a show,
Where mischievous mice steal the glow.
They squeak and dart in silly sprints,
Turning shadows into hints.

In every nook, a jest unfolds,
Nature's humor, pure and bold.
Beneath the trees, the laughter swells,
In soft embraces where silliness dwells!

The Tender Quiet of the Woods

Underneath a blanket green,
A fox wears shoes that shine and gleam.
He struts along the winding path,
While birds all chuckle in their bath.

A bear attempts the waltz, you see,
With bumblebees as company.
He trips and rolls; they buzz in shock,
And sprinkle honey on a rock.

Frogs on logs create a band,
Playing tunes so wildly grand.
Their concerts draw the deer and hare,
Who prance around without a care.

Laughter floats on dappled light,
As creatures join the frolic night.
Nature's joy, a grand parade,
In tender whispers, fun is made!

Green Dreams in Twilight

In the forest where shadows dance,
Frogs wear slippers, they prance.
They leap and croak a silly song,
Chasing fireflies all night long.

Squirrels trade nuts for a smile,
Raccoons dance in a funny style.
The trees giggle with each breeze,
While the owls hoot, 'Avert your eyes, please!'

At dusk the ants throw a big ball,
With pompoms made from leaves, oh so small.
The moon winks with a cheerful glow,
As crickets play their tunes, row after row.

Dreams of green fill the air,
Where laughter blossoms everywhere.
A playful breeze lifts spirits high,
In this realm where silliness shall never die.

Twilight's Gentle Embrace

In the gentle hush of dusk,
Bats don capes, a sight to trust.
Chasing mosquitoes in a game,
Calling out, 'Catch me!' with no shame.

A turtle goes for a speedy stroll,
Hitching a ride on a wise old mole.
They swap tales of their slower days,
While the fireflies light up in a blaze.

Lemurs laugh as they swing around,
Upside down, they revel and clown.
The shadows stretch, their faces bright,
While the stars above twinkle with delight.

A parade of laughter fills the scene,
As nature's misfits are dressed up in green.
In twilight's embrace, joy takes flight,
And everything feels just perfect tonight.

Murmuring Mists of Dawn

As dawn breaks with a golden hue,
The raccoons put on their morning shoe.
With a yawn and stretch, they greet the day,
While a sloth rolls over, still wants to play.

The mist giggles, whispers a tune,
A chorus of critters beneath the moon.
The butterflies wear skirts made of dew,
And ants march in line, a marching crew.

Silly monkeys swing from vine to vine,
Their chatter rings sweet like aged wine.
A frog in a top hat hops by with flair,
'Turn to the left!' he shouts with a stare.

Morning's light, a canvas so bright,
Where every creature finds pure delight.
In the mist, laughter floats around,
In this hilarious world, joy is found.

Peace in the Hidden Depths

In depths where secrets softly sleep,
The fish wear hats, far from the deep.
With bubbles that tickle and twist in glee,
They swim in circles, a silly spree.

Turtles play hide and seek with the reeds,
While shrimp boost their self-esteem with some speeds.
The crabs have a party by the sandy shore,
Dancing with shells till they can't dance anymore.

A lazy catfish floats, a true charmer,
With a grin, he's quite the swimmer's armor.
He tells tall tales of oceans vast,
While guppies giggle, they're having a blast.

Underwater peace reigns without stress,
As laughter bubbles in water's caress.
In these hidden realms, fun takes the lead,
Where every splash is a comic deed.

Secrets Among the Ferns

In leafy greens where whispers hide,
A squirrel's joke takes us for a ride.
Frogs laugh deep in their squishy throne,
Crafting puns in their croaky tone.

Twirling vines with winks and grins,
A sloth's slow dance, where patience wins.
Parrots squawk with a comic flair,
Even the bugs join in this affair.

Murmurs in the Underbrush

Bumbling bees in mismatched socks,
Buzzing secrets from leafy blocks.
Beneath the fronds, a gossip fest,
Each critter trying to crack the jest.

Lizards lounging, sharing memes,
Chasing shadows, fulfilling dreams.
The beat of drums from caverns deep,
While sleepy sloths just want more sleep.

Echoes of Solitude

In stillness where the shadows play,
A lone raccoon recounts his day.
He finds a twig, a makeshift mic,
Telling tales of a late-night hike.

Mice tap dance on a silver leaf,
While chattering birds provide belief.
A lazy armadillo rolls on by,
Wondering if he should just fly.

Hidden Harmonies of the Wild

Underneath the ferns, a tune,
Composed by crickets in a swoon.
A tortoise nods to the funky beat,
As ants march on with tiny feet.

Hummingbirds hum to the rhythm right,
Dancing shadows in the fading light.
Jungle laughter fills the air,
A symphony of joy everywhere.

Nature's Soft Serenade

Whispers dance in leafy halls,
Where chattering critters share their calls.
A frog in sunglasses jumps with glee,
Croaking tunes of a wild jubilee.

Squirrels trading jokes in the trees,
While the sloths take naps with lazy ease.
A raccoon wears a hat, quite bizarre,
Declaring himself the jungle's star.

Lizards laugh with colorful flair,
As flowers giggle, losing their hair.
The breeze joins in, a playful tune,
Nature's laughter beneath the moon.

So if you're lost in this leafy maze,
Join in the fun, let your heart blaze!
For even in shadows where creatures reside,
The jungle's a party where joy can't hide.

Muffled Heartbeats in the Thicket

In the thicket, secrets sway,
Where squirrels clash in a nutty fray.
A peacock struts in a plume parade,
Exclaiming loudly, "I'm not afraid!"

Bouncing bunnies, in comical hops,
Tell tall tales of their last mishaps.
The turtles race, their shells weigh a ton,
Yet every race is all in good fun.

A babbling brook says, "Take a sip!"
With the fish wearing ties, it's a classy trip.
While butterflies flirt and drift through the day,
Chasing dreams in a whimsical way.

In every rustle, a chuckle's concealed,
Nature's humor oh so revealed.
So tiptoe softly and join the jest,
In the thicket, laughter is the best.

Tales from the Murmuring Brush

Beneath the ferns, critters convene,
With stories of adventures unseen.
A fox in a bowtie shares his lore,
Of how he snagged a dance with a door!

The whispers of leaves hold giggling dreams,
As antelopes plot their silly schemes.
A beaver with glasses whittles away,
While the owls hoot jokes at the end of the day.

A chameleon boasts of colors he's worn,
While munching on snacks, all freshly shorn.
Rabbits recount their wildest leaps,
While the wise old pig snores in deep sleeps.

In the brush where the breezes swirl,
The laughter of nature begins to unfurl.
So gather around, let the tales abound,
Where humor in whispers can always be found.

The Solace of Silhouette

In twilight's glow, shadows play,
Chasing winks of the fading day.
A panther prances in moonlit attire,
As crickets strum in a quirky choir.

A sloth on a branch, takes a selfie,
While the fireflies buzz, feeling healthy.
The shadows chuckle, in shapes they bend,
All laughter together, it has no end.

The owls hoot a giggly refrain,
As freshly cut grass embraces the rain.
A shadowy fox crafts tricks with finesse,
Playing hide and seek in a whimsical dress.

So when night falls and silhouettes bloom,
Join the ruckus, banish the gloom.
For in the solace of twilight's embrace,
Even shadows dance with a smile on their face.

Whispers of Life in Shadows

In the shade where monkeys swing,
A parrot squawks, what fun it brings!
The sloth rolls by, slow and sly,
Waving to the bugs that fly.

Tigers nap in midday light,
Dreaming of their next delight.
A frog leaps high, with quite the splash,
While crickets hold a silly bash!

Down below, the ants parade,
In tiny hats, they're all arrayed.
With little drums, they march in sync,
To the rhythm of a puddle's blink.

Crocodiles with toothy grins,
Play peekaboo; the game begins!
While butterflies dance in the breeze,
Twirling round with utmost ease.

Nature's Quiet Soliloquy

In a leafy nook where shadows play,
A cheeky squirrel stole my clay.
He said with glee, 'Now I shall mold!'
Then rolled away, so bold, so bold!

A startled deer jumps back in fright,
At a breathy end to morning's light.
But then he trips over his own shoes,
And in the mud, he makes the news!

The birds in chatter, gossip low,
About the howler's latest show.
He thinks he's loud, a real rock star,
But all he gets is a rubber jar!

Even flowers dress in laughter bright,
With petals waving, what a sight!
While grasshoppers tax their clever minds,
With silly rhymes that no one finds.

Choreography of Stillness

In a field where zephyrs tease,
A shy tortoise seeks some cheese.
He dreams of running, oh so fast,
But with each step, he's outclassed!

A chameleon in a fashion spree,
Changes hues for all to see.
Yet slips on leaves, takes a tumble,
Then grins and chuckles, not a mumble!

Frogs in tuxedos prance about,
With tiny canes, no hint of doubt.
They leap and bow, then strike a pose,
While the lizards laugh, strike silly throes.

It's a serenade of bemused quirks,
Where nature's laughter always works.
Underneath the timorous guise,
Life still twirls in sweet surprise.

The Pacing of Gentle Time

The brook gurgles with a cheeky grin,
While skipping stones dance and spin.
The fish roll over, smirking wide,
Winking at the frogs who glide.

An elephant breaks to do the twist,
And all the critters stop to assist.
With a swing and a sway, they gather near,
Join the groove without a fear!

A beetle drums on a fallen log,
Rallying pals, it's quite a fog!
The monkeys cheer, with high-five flair,
In harmony, they leap through air!

As dusk draws in with gentle sighs,
The moon peeks out with sleepy eyes.
While fireflies wink, a starry mime,
In this symphony, we sway with time.

The Whispering Wilderness

In the woods where squirrels play,
The trees gossip night and day.
Frogs narrate tales with glee,
While rabbits plot the next big spree.

A bear wears socks, bright and pink,
Sipping tea, he's had a drink.
Chasing butterflies with flair,
He trips on roots, oh what a scare!

The shadows dance, they tease the light,
A raccoon steals cookies at midnight.
All the critters break out in song,
As the owl hums along, right or wrong.

With every rustle, laughter bursts,
Each creature's joke, it truly thirsts.
In this realm of chitter and cheer,
What's serious? Not a thing here!

Echoes of Ancient Roots

Underneath the big old tree,
A turtle's losing his grand key.
The root's wriggling like a snake,
And the ants cheer for goodness' sake!

A wise old owl in specs so round,
Cracks jokes that simply astound.
With every hoot, the forest shakes,
As laughter responses the ground wakes.

Silly shadows creep and crawl,
Chasing each other, they trip and fall.
The vines laugh and sway with glee,
While crickets boast, 'Come dance with me!'

Every echo tells a tale,
Of goofy ghosts and a dancing snail.
In this land where fun is king,
Even stones can dance and sing!

The Lullaby of Leaves

The leaves start humming a soft tune,
Under the watch of a sleepy moon.
A fox in pajamas, quite absurd,
Attempts to whistle with a fuzzy bird.

The breeze tickles the branches wide,
Making the flowers giggle, can't hide.
A hiccup from a sloth up high,
Sends acorns tumbling from the sky.

The midnight raccoons, a band of three,
Play on drums made of honey and tree.
Every thud makes the squirrels dance,
While the snoring bear joins in the chance.

Yet, when dawn breaks with a yawn,
The silliness fades with the lawn.
But come nightfall, oh what a sight,
The jungle is ready for another delight!

Beneath the Silent Boughs

Under tall trees, spies gather 'round,
A brigade of ants, oh what a sound!
Planning a feast for the dusk-timed show,
With crumbs from the picnic, they'll surely glow.

A chattering parrot steals the stage,
With jokes that could start a new age.
Chipmunks giggle at his funny squawks,
As he juggles nuts and hops like a fox.

In this realm where laughter grows,
A hedgehog prances in mismatched clothes.
Every twirl, a delightful cheer,
In the night, silliness draws near!

When shadows stretch and the stars align,
The critters sit down with mugs of brine.
By the light of the moon, they find their groove,
In a silent dance that just can't lose!

Hush of the Night Bloom

In the dark, a frog sings loud,
His croaks attract the sleepy crowd.
Fireflies dance with a flicker bright,
While owls pretend they're out of sight.

A hedgehog rolls into a ball,
He thinks he's hidden, thinks he's small.
But a raccoon with a cheeky grin,
Counters with antics, ready to win.

The moonlight casts a silver glow,
As chatter fills the night below.
Silly whispers, grinning snakes,
Jesting with humor, for laughter's sake.

So join the fun, embrace the glee,
In the leaves where joy runs free.
Night blooms open, revealing cheer,
With creatures laughing, never fear.

Guardians of the Silent Grove

Beneath the trees, a sloth takes a nap,
While squirrels plan a mischief trap.
Raccoons plotting with stars in their eyes,
Chasing each other for tasty fries.

The wise old owl gives a stern look,
But a kid with mischief reads a book.
Snapping branches, a great big scare,
Laughter erupts; it's a jungle affair.

The turtles race, though slow and stuck,
Yet cheer them on, they'll change their luck.
A hedgehog rolls, fast as can be,
"Who needs speed when you've got glee?"

Together they dance, under the moon,
Chasing shadows, they hum a tune.
Guardians smile as fun takes flight,
In the serene, silly, starry night.

Enigmatic Beings in the Thicket

In the thicket, a monkey swings,
Juggling fruits, oh, what fun it brings!
A parrot shouts, 'Catch me if you can!'
While a turtle grins, 'I'm still your fan.'

Secret meetings under the vine,
Deer in pajamas sipping fine wine.
All the while, the crickets play,
Making music until the break of day.

A chameleon chuckles, shifts his face,
While a hummingbird zooms all over the place.
"Hey, slow down!" calls a witty goat,
"Let's keep this party afloat, let's gloat!"

With cozy whispers of tickling breeze,
All creatures gather, just to tease.
In the thicket, smiles abound,
Where mysterious laughter can always be found.

Petals of Peace

From a flower, a gentle breeze blows,
Spreading joy where nobody knows.
A butterfly winks with colors so bright,
While a bear shares cookies, oh what a sight!

The wise old fox tells riddles and tales,
As laughter blooms, no one fails.
A parade of ants marches with pride,
Carrying crumbs, a feast to confide.

In the calm of the green, the chortles rise,
With giggles echoing through the skies.
Petals flutter, soft and sweet,
As friends gather round, with food to eat.

Under the stars, all sit at ease,
Spreading joy like petals in the breeze.
In this stillness, humor takes flight,
Petals of peace, in the warm moonlight.

Whispers in the Canopy

The monkeys chatter with glee,
Telling jokes from tree to tree.
A parrot squawks a trendy line,
While sloths just hang, entwined with twine.

A toucan struts in bright display,
Says, "Who needs work? Let's just play!"
Yet as they giggle high and low,
The jaguar snores, and dreams of snow.

In shadows, ants throw tiny raves,
Gossiping about the local faves.
While frogs croak tunes, a rhythmic beat,
They dance around with hopping feet.

Amidst the laughs, a breeze does sway,
As laughter lingers, bright and gay.
In this green realm, so wild and free,
Nature's humor is the ticket, you see!

Shadows Beneath the Leaves

The breeze tickles the ferns so sweet,
While critters play a game of hide-and-seek.
A lizard slips, then strikes a pose,
As if he's starring in a show, who knows?

A squirrel shares his nutty jokes,
And warns the others of sneaky folks.
"I saw a snake trying hard to mime,
But all he got was tangled in time!"

In dappled light, the beetles roll,
Looking for snacks to fill their bowl.
With every crack, a giggle grows,
A sergeant ant says, "This is how it goes!"

Yet through the fun, a turtle scrapes,
"Slow your roll, or miss the shapes!
We'll laugh and play till the sun sets low,
Then back to work, so off we'll go!

Silence Among the Vines

Among the vines, a sloth so slow,
Wakes up and says, "Hey, let's go!"
But all his friends remain asleep,
"Too tired, dear friend, the world can keep!"

A chameleon shows off his new hue,
Says, "I changed for you, no, more like two!"
He trips on roots and lands with flair,
The laughter echoes, fills the air.

A witty snake, with tales so grand,
Says, "You won't believe what's in this land!"
But all they hear is a sleepy sigh,
As he curls up with a simple "Bye!"

And still the jungle laughs and ponders,
While sleepy heads avoid all wonders.
But in their hearts, the fun is there,
In leafy shades, they simply care!

Veils of Green Stillness

'Twas a calm morn in the backdrop lush,
When frogs decided to make a rush.
"Leap with style!" one shouted loud,
And landed splat! It drew a crowd.

An iguana yawns; what's this craze?
He shakes his head in a lazy daze.
"Just hop along, don't make a fuss,
Life's too short; let's ride the bus!"

A tiny bug joins with a tune,
Twisting in dance beneath the moon.
But all the while, it trips and falls,
"Why do I dance? I'll hit the walls!"

Yet through the stillness, laughter roams,
With nature's echoes, joy finds homes.
In veils of green, the jesters play,
All under the sun's warm, golden ray!

Murmurs in the Underbrush

Whispers flutter, leaves collide,
A squirrel's giggle, it cannot hide.
A sneaky frog in muddy shoes,
Croaks jokes loud, then slyly snooze.

Vines tangle up, in playful tease,
The parrot cackles, dancing with ease.
A lizard slips, tongue in a twist,
Spills the beans, then shakes his fist.

Butterflies flutter with silly grace,
One trips and lands right on my face!
I laugh aloud, the jungle roars,
Nature's quirks open playful doors.

In the shade, the fun won't stop,
A sloth hangs low, takes a nap drop.
Yet every creature shares a jest,
In this realm, we're all a guest.

The Stillness of Emerald Deep

In emerald greenery, joy unfolds,
With animals plotting, stories told.
A monkey swings, oh-so-slick,
Who knew bananas could be such a trick?

A toucan's beak, a playful show,
Bright colors clash, putting on a glow.
While turtles waddle, slow parade,
Around the pond, their plans are laid.

Giggling frogs in a muddy row,
Compete in jumps, they steal the show.
One did a flip, the others yawned,
"Let's just stick to the ground," they responded.

In this lush realm where laughter breathes,
Every bush hides a joke beneath leaves.
Nature's packed with humor galore,
Secrets tumble out with roars.

Secrets Beneath the Foliage

Beneath the leaves, where chuckles nest,
A raccoon plots its latest quest.
"Steal the picnic? What a delight!"
But tripping over a root, it took flight.

The vines twist tight, a prankster's snare,
With monkeys swinging, laughter in the air.
One lost a hat, and oh, the drama!
His pals erupted in sweet comedrama!

In silence, creepers share a grin,
A snake in shades enjoys the din.
He hisses puns, and then he writhes,
While chameleons laugh, changing their lives.

Beetles boast of great escapades,
While beetle dances steal the glades.
Each rustle tells a tale anew,
In this playful world, we all accrue.

Hushed Echoes of Nature

In hushed tones, the woodland sings,
A turtle serenades with poppin' blings.
While owls hoot an unexpected pun,
They've got the wisdom, but also the fun!

Flitting fairies play tag with light,
Stumbling fireflies, a glowing sight.
A moose with shades struts down the path,
Who knew the forest had such a laugh?

Crazy crickets throw a dance bash,
While ants join in, moving with panache.
A party of critters, wild and free,
Even a bear says, "Let's all agree!"

Every corner hums with giggling cheer,
As squirrels debate who steals the pear.
In this hush, a loud delight,
Nature's humor takes flight at night.

Serene Shadows of the Realm

In the midst of leaves so lush,
A spider spins his webs with glee,
He plans a party, oh so grand,
Inviting all from land to tree.

But ants march in with clumsy feet,
A conga line of six and more,
They knock down snacks, the feast's a mess,
While squirrels laugh and search for more.

The sloths hang low, their eyes half-closed,
They groove so slow with leafy vibes,
While parrot tells the silliest joke,
And all the critters take their bribes.

Yet in this haze of funny fun,
The moon peeks in, a silver grin,
The jungle's heartbeat, soft and swift,
A place where laughter can begin.

Restful Retreats of the Earth

Beneath the ferns, a turtle snores,
He dreams of races, oh what speed!
While crickets chirp their own night tunes,
Trying to be the dance floor's lead.

A chameleon hops, all out of whack,
Changing colors just to be seen,
A party crasher, no it's not,
Just looking for the best cuisine.

The hedge-bugs brew their silly tea,
While fireflies flicker like tiny ships,
They sail through dreams on gentle streams,
Creating nightlights for their trips.

Yet even here, with all the fun,
The shadows sneak and swirl with cheer,
A giggle echoes through the dark,
Whispers of wonder, hugs of fear.

The Cacophony of Calm

In the cat-owl's silent hoot,
A chorus of frogs croak in tone,
They gather round, a talent show,
Where dreams of fame are often sown.

The fireflies judge, with sparks in eyes,
As toads go on with duo acts,
A prankster lizard steals the show,
With wacky moves and funny quacks.

The rustling leaves can't handle it,
They chuckle low, a gentle breeze,
As whispers bounce among the trees,
A giggling dance to please the bees.

A slithering snake can't join the fun,
But cheers him on, they all agree,
That laughter's best, and with a grin,
They cheer each act in jubilee!

In the Heart of Stillness

In a nook where frogs play chess,
The air is thick with thoughts of crabs,
Who joke about the size of shells,
As turtles laugh with honey-babs.

A wise old owl sits up so tall,
He throws down cards, but can't recall,
The rules of poker in the dusk,
As shadows dance and jitter-bug.

The vines will sway, a funky beat,
As beetles shake their ruffled coats,
In this calm, a cheerful thrum,
Gives even grumpy cats their gloats.

In stillness, secrets twirl around,
The jungle's humor knows no end,
From whispers to a hearty giggle,
It's all the joy the critters send.

Secrets of the Emerald Glade

In deepest shades where shadows play,
The chameleon's dance steals your gaze,
With colors that shift like a fancy hat,
He chuckles softly, 'Look at that!'

A sloth hangs down from a leafy bough,
Sipping tea from his own brow,
He waves with a yawn, says, 'What's the rush?'
While iguanas laugh, causing quite a hush.

The frogs wear coats of polished sheen,
Croaking tunes, a humorous scene,
One leaps up high, slips in the mud,
Yet jumps back out with a zany thud!

Beneath the canopy where secrets hum,
The tortoise grins, 'I'm just not dumb,'
He whispers tales of the world so wide,
While the busy ants stomp down with pride.

Solitary Dwellers of the Light

A lone owl, wise with stunning flair,
Glares at the raccoon with a puzzled stare,
'Why so much fuss with your trashy game?'
Raccoon shrugs, 'The fame, my friend, the fame!'

The fireflies wink in mischievous play,
Guiding the lost on their silly way,
'Tap your feet!' they giggle in flight,
'Join our dance, we'll light up the night!'

In shadows thick, the mongooses squirm,
With grand plans to kidnap a worm,
'Hey, it's lunch!' they chuckle and tease,
As a snake slithers by with stealthy ease.

The jaguar paces, sleek and sly,
Mocking the monkeys who swing and cry,
'You think that's a call? Poor, poor belay,'
While the monkeys just cackle, 'That's our way!'

Breathing Life into Silence

Whispers of breezes and leaflets rustle,
The quiet frog holds a leafy hustle,
He puffs his cheeks, croaks just for fun,
'That's my solo, aren't I the one?'

A hidden squirrel, a jittery chap,
Picks up an acorn, gives a quick clap,
With a classic misstep, he tumbles round,
And the forest erupts in a giggling sound.

The trees bend low in a silent cheer,
To the shy parrot who's growing near,
'Watch me mimic, with flair and guile,'
But ends up sounding like a goofy style.

A sleeping chameleon snores like a truck,
Spraying colors like he's just out of luck,
While the ants pass by, take heed of its shade,
'Look at our pal, in dreams he's obeyed!'

Stillness Wrapped in Green

Among the leaves, the monkeys dwell,
Playing tag with a soft, sweet smell,
They trip on vines, fall into a heap,
Bursting with laughter, they go back to sleep.

Lizards sunbathe on rocks so grand,
Bragging proudly about their tan,
But when a crow caws, they all scatter,
Yelling, 'Who invited him? What's the matter?'

The vines entwine in gossip galore,
As the snails glide slowly, always wanting more,
They sip on dew, and ponder a race,
'At this rate, we'll win! Let's pick up the pace!'

With rustling leaves and shy critters near,
Life in green is just full of cheer,
Every whisper and giggle adrift,
In this forest of fun, the spirits uplift.

Dappled Sunlight's Embrace

In the woods where shadows play,
A squirrel thinks it's a ballet.
Chasing sunbeams, oh what joy!
A dance-off with a sneaky boy.

The tree limbs giggle in the breeze,
While ants debate on greatest cheese.
A butterfly slips on a leaf,
Yelling, 'I've turned into a thief!'

Snakes wear ties in a funny way,
While frogs practice for a cabaret.
The beetles clink their tiny cups,
And ants join in for fancy ups.

With laughter echoing so bright,
Nature holds a fun-filled night.
Each creature shares a silly grin,
In this woodland, joy won't thin.

Where the Wild Things Pause

In the bramble, a lion yawns,
Dreaming he's wearing golden fawns.
Nearby, a monkey paints his toe,
While giraffes giggle, 'Look at that show!'

A porcupine wrote a long book,
Its cover's made from a hidden nook.
Vultures host a comedic play,
While rabbits hop and bounce away.

Hippos snort in splendid tune,
Dancing wildly under the moon.
A chameleon wears a bright hat,
Pretending he's got a chubby cat.

Where wild things pause, the laughter's loud,
From furry friends to the stillness proud.
Here humor reigns without a fight,
Nature's jesters bringing delight.

The Lullaby of the Wild

Crickets croon their nighttime song,
As owls hoot, 'You can't go wrong!'
A raccoon fluffs its fluffy tail,
Singing soft notes that surely sail.

The fireflies dance with blinking light,
Teaching worms how to twirl at night.
A sloth pretends it's flying high,
With dreams of racing through the sky.

Mice form bands with tiny drums,
While hedgehogs roll, the rhythm comes.
Each creature hums a tune so sweet,
Making midnight moments a treat.

The lullaby makes all things stay,
In gentle whispers, they must play.
Here cheeky smiles and fun collide,
Under starlit skies, take a ride.

Tranquil Heart of the Forest

In the forest where the sun peeks,
A fox teaches the bear to speak.
They trade puns with a wise-bird's song,
Creating laughs all day long!

Bamboo giggles when pandas slide,
Just like the breeze in nature's glide.
Shy turtles play hide and seek,
While elephants stomp with exuberant squeaks.

Monkeys juggle bananas with flair,
While frogs leap high without a care.
The trees whisper secrets so sly,
As critters dance and spirits fly.

In this heart where laughter swells,
Each tale of joy the forest tells.
Nature's embrace, a buoyant spark,
Where humor blooms and lights the dark.

Serenade of the Hidden Ones

In shadows deep, the critters play,
With chirps and squeaks, they steal the day.
A squirrel in a hat, what a sight,
Trying to dance, oh what a fright!

The frogs croak tunes, a grand delight,
While raccoons sing under the moonlight.
A toucan drops jokes from above,
In this giggling green, we all feel love.

The snakes do slither with a twist,
Making up songs that can't be missed.
A chameleon croons in colors bright,
Changing the mood with pure delight!

So come join the fun, don't be shy,
In leafy cover, let your heart fly.
With laughter and cheer, the hidden ones sing,
In the secret realm where joy is king.

Reflection in the Shaded Glade

In glades so wide, the shadows dance,
A turtle teeters in a goofy prance.
A parrot squawks, "I can't find my hat!"
While a lazy sloth naps, what of that?

The trees lean in, like tipsy friends,
Eavesdropping on the chatter that never ends.
A mischievous monkey swings with glee,
Sipping on nectar, "What's next for me?"

A butterfly winks in sparkling hues,
As beetles boast about their best shoes.
With laughter echoing through the tie,
Sunshine beams, and the days flit by.

In this shady arcade, come join the show,
With giggles and thrills, our spirits will grow.
So dance with the shadows, let stories unfold,
In the glade where fun is bought, not sold.

The Breath of Ancient Trees

The ancient giants sway and creak,
Whispering tales of the cheeky meek.
A wise old owl with spectacles round,
Quotes Shakespeare while perched on the ground.

The vines are tangled, forming a jest,
A hammock for frogs who just want to rest.
They dream of flies dressed smart and bright,
In flights of fancy, oh what a sight!

Lizards flip coins on the mossy stone,
Betting on leaves that swirl and moan.
While squirrels debate the best peanut stash,
In this leafy world, we laugh and dash.

With branches shaking in glee, they agree,
That humor's the fruit from every tree.
So breathe it in, let the fun begin,
In the depths of green where the chuckles spin.

Muffled Steps in the Heartwood

In the heart of woods, where whispers creep,
Funny footsteps sprinkle, then leap.
A rabbit tripped, fluff flew in the air,
Bunny ballet? More like a dare!

The shadows giggle, the moon sneers bright,
As bushes gossip about late-night flight.
A fox, quite dapper, pulls off a bow,
While squirrels roll laughter—OH NO, NOT NOW!

The owls hoot gossip from high above,
While insects sing sweetly, a glimmer of love.
An awkward turtle shuffles too far,
Stepping on mushrooms like a true rock star!

So wander the paths, take a step slow,
In the heartwood giggles, let comedy flow.
With each muffled step, let the delight grow,
In this forest fun, let your heart glow.

Serendipity Among the Vines

Beneath the leaves, a monkey grins,
A feathered hat and clumsy spins.
He trips on roots, does a silly dance,
While lizards stare, in jest they prance.

The sloths are laughing, oh what a sight,
As squirrels gossip from morning till night.
A tangle of vines, a playful snare,
Where every critter finds a reason to share.

A toucan toasts with a ripe, juicy fruit,
While ants parade in their tiny suit.
They march in lines, but lose their way,
Chasing shadows in a bright cabaret.

Amid green giants, mischief abounds,
With giggles and grumbles, joy resounds.
In this leafy world, craziness reigns,
A serendipitous romp with no constraints.

The Veil of Verdant Hush

In a grove where crickets croon,
A sloth plays tunes with a rusty spoon.
The bushy-tailed critters join the fun,
As butterfly dancers twirl in the sun.

A parrot's squawk causes quite a scene,
As capybaras lounge, oh so serene.
They crack jokes about the dewdrop's fall,
In harmony, they share their wittiest call.

Beneath the shade, a turtle slips,
Into a prank, he playfully trips.
With a chuckle, he turns to say,
"Who knew muddy was the brand today?"

In this realm, the laughter thrives,
Amidst the calm, the spirit drives.
Each laughter echoes, thus it sneaks,
A joke here or there, this jungle speaks.

Tranquility's Hidden Path

Along the trail, the giggles bloom,
A rabbit hops, and stamps the room.
With every bounce, there's a little cheer,
As frogs join in, crooning without fear.

The shadows sway as if they're alive,
Where chattering monkeys just can't survive.
Caught in a game of hide and seek,
In all the rustle, it's all quite unique.

A lost toucan can't find his way,
He wears a hat – oh, what a display!
With every flap, he looks so bold,
Yet the maze of leaves never gets old.

In secret corners, secrets run deep,
Where whispers of giggles break the sleep.
Amidst the calm, mischief takes flight,
With joy and laughter, pure delight.

A Serenade of Still Life

The painters sing under a big old tree,
As ants line up with cups of tea.
A hedgehog butler, quite the chap,
Serves pastries made from nature's wrap.

It seems the flowers sway with glee,
While a clumsy bear attempts to flee.
He trips on roots, and oh, what a fall,
A cascade of petals, covering all.

The turtles play chess, slow but witty,
While everyone else finds it all quite Pity.
They laugh at clouds drifting so high,
As the sun winks, watching from the sky.

In this still life, chaque crêature,
Leads their roles with a dance and stature.
Mirth and giggles blend with the sight,
In nature's art, a canvas of light.

www.ingramcontent.com/pod-product-compliance
Lightning Source LLC
Chambersburg PA
CBHW072121070526
44585CB00016B/1522